Praise for *Building Wea*

"Building Wealth For 7
sponsibility and securit

— John Gleeson, age 20

"Building Wealth For Teens is a well written book that provides an introduction to many financial concepts and topics of interest to teenagers...the most valuable part of the book is advice Matheson gives...in which he sets out a philosophy and view of the world with which we all agree but sometimes forget."

— Mark Wolynetz Ph.D, CFP, ChFC, CLU

"This book was very informative...clarified many things I was unsure of...many great explanations and examples...I highly recommend it."

— Mark Boschman, age 19

"Murdoch Matheson takes the complexities of financial planning out of the equation and presents a simple, relevant, concrete foundation upon which youth may begin to assume their own role in securing their financial future."

— Frank Wiley, Principal, Canterbury High School,

Ottawa, Ontario

"I loved how the book was short and to the point...perfect for someone my age or younger...great introduction to these topics."

— Mark Sullivan, age 19

"Building Wealth For Teens is a wonderful read...The author has demonstrated a real skill for transforming complicated topics into easy to understand terms that anyone, young or old, can easily appreciate... With its straight-to-the-point approach, this book should be essential reading for every teenager who wants to learn more about the financial world we all live in."

— Jeffery Keill, CFP, CIM

Building Wealth
For
TEENS

Answers To Questions Teens Care About

MURDOCH MATHESON

Order this book online at www.trafford.com/05-3051
or email orders@trafford.com

Most Trafford titles are also available at major online book retailers.

Note for Librarians: A cataloguing record for this book is available from Library
and Archives Canada at www.collectionscanada.ca/amicus/index-e.html

Printed in Victoria, BC, Canada.

ISBN: 978-1-4120-8053-8

*We at Trafford believe that it is the responsibility of us all, as both individuals
and corporations, to make choices that are environmentally and socially sound.
You, in turn, are supporting this responsible conduct each time you purchase a
Trafford book, or make use of our publishing services. To find out how you are
helping, please visit www.trafford.com/responsiblepublishing.html*

*Our mission is to efficiently provide the world's finest, most comprehensive
book publishing service, enabling every author to experience success.
To find out how to publish your book, your way, and have it available
worldwide, visit us online at www.trafford.com/10510*

 www.trafford.com

North America & international
toll-free: 1 888 232 4444 (USA & Canada)
phone: 250 383 6864 ♦ fax: 250 383 6804 ♦ email: info@trafford.com

The United Kingdom & Europe
phone: +44 (0)1865 722 113 ♦ local rate: 0845 230 9601
facsimile: +44 (0)1865 722 868 ♦ email: info.uk@trafford.com

10 9 8 7 6

Acknowledgements

Back in 2000, when my older son Brock was in grade eight at A. Lorne Cassidy School in Stittsville, Ontario, he was fortunate to have a wonderful teacher by the name of Mrs. Karen Deurloo. I approached Mrs. Deurloo with the idea that it would be valuable and instructive to hear from grade eight students, as they began their teen years, on various topics including money, investments and building wealth (to name a few). These questions, which formed the titles of the book chapters, were possible thanks to Mrs. Deurloo, who allowed access to her two classes. She was encouraging in her support for this project aimed at building teen financial and investment literacy. Mrs. Deurloo offered editorial guidance as well, which was most appreciated.

I'd like to thank Gail Baird of Creative Bound Inc. who provided editorial guidance.

Sid Tafler's editorial and marketing advice and support has been invaluable.

Sons Brock, Ian and their friends, Brent Boschman and Mark Sullivan were all very helpful in their role as consultants for the book, addressing size, shape and cover content which proved most helpful. Ian advised me on the computer work associated with preparing the text for publication. I am grateful to these individuals for their important assistance.

I want to thank Steve McLean for his feedback and advice regarding applications for this book project.

The support of my wife Mary Jane and sons Brock and Ian made this book possible. It is dedicated to Brock, Ian and their fellow classmates who are living through their teen years, a special phase of their lives that they will remember fondly.

Building Wealth For Teens

Contents

Introduction

In our technology-driven world, young people (and the rest of us too!) are bombarded with instant information overload on every imaginable subject. At times it is difficult to sift through it all and find a simple explanation to specific areas of interest. As students in school, today's youth are exposed to many useful and interesting course topics, including business and economics but precious few, if any, on personal finance. This is the focus of this book project.

As a certified financial planner who has worked with families and youth for years, I have noted that there is a significant gap in knowledge where teens are concerned, in terms of financial and investment literacy. At the same time, I was seeking a unique approach where teens wouldn't feel lectured to, as if they were taking another course in school. For this book to work it had to be guided by students, capturing the essence of particular topics supplied by teens, in a few short, easy reading pages. Each chapter had to be brief, non-technical and conversational for teens to be motivated to read. This was the basis upon which this project came alive, drawing the questions (and chapter titles) from two classes of teens taught by Mrs. Karen Deurloo at A. Lorne Cassidy School in Stittsville, Ontario.

My hope is that this book will ignite a spark of interest and lifelong learning on topics about money, financial security and wealth-building so that young people, as they move forward with their lives, will have the comfort and freedom to focus on the things that really matter.

1

What Is Income?

Income is money paid to you in return for something. Babysitting your neighbour's children or cutting their grass results in a few dollars coming your way. An allowance from your parents or birthday or Christmas gift money also may be considered income. The money you make from a part-time or full-time job represents income. All of these represent money coming to you.

Most people think of income as a regular stream of money coming to them from a part-time or regular job. Working at a local restaurant or business means you'll be receiving regular cash or cheques. As you get older and take on a full-time job, the money or income you receive will take on greater meaning as your 'wish list' grows for things you'd like to own or acquire.

There are two interesting sides to income. One is that you have a right to receive a fair wage or income for the work that you do. After all, life costs money and you need only review your 'wish list' for that point to hit home.

The other side is more complex. It is that you have a responsibility to use your income wisely. Why? It is very easy to spend money or income and have nothing left over to address your continuing needs. And we all have continuing, unending needs of one sort or another, many of which have to do with money. Parents try their best to help their children appreciate that money should be managed carefully. As nice as the idea sounds, money really doesn't grow on trees. We have a responsibility to ourselves and the people we love to be smart with our income.

What does being smart with our income mean? Here are a few brief points to consider about using income wisely.

- Try to spend less than you earn, every cheque, every month.
- Invest a part of every cheque for your future and/or retirement needs. You can never start an investment program too soon. Time is by far the most

important factor in building enough money for your future security, so don't squander it by not acting early enough.

- Set money aside for your personal daily discretionary spending – fun money, vacation, whatever. Striking a balance between planning ahead and enjoying every day is important.
- Be aware that earned income (and other forms of income from investments) are taxable if your overall income exceeds a certain minimum level, so money should be set aside for taxes unless your income is taxed by your employer at source.
- Consider giving to a charity where you may direct a portion of every cheque you earn. This single initiative may give you a lifetime of fulfillment, knowing you are making a positive difference in other peoples' lives.

2

How Often
Do You Have to Pay a Bill?

It's easier to tackle this topic if we first define what we mean by the word 'bill'.

When you receive a product or service, there is usually a cost for that exchange that we call an invoice or bill. When you go to the local store, you pay the cashier for the gum or candy you bought. Paying bills works much the same way.

We receive a monthly bill or invoice for many services we receive in our everyday lives. This list usually includes:

- telephone/internet
- cable TV
- water
- heat
- electricity
- credit card bills (for regular purchases)
- mortgage (paying for our home)
- car costs

Most often these bills arrive by mail or on our computer via the Internet and we are expected to write cheques or transfer money, typically from a bank, to pay for them.

Some bills, like government taxes (for government services), are paid on your behalf by your employer. Or you may arrange for taxes to be paid quarterly or annually, but most bills are paid monthly.

If you choose not to pay certain bills (for example, credit card charges) when they're due, you will usually incur extra charges (called interest) on top of the original billed amount.

The cost of your entire lifestyle determines how expensive your bills will be each month. There are many factors that go into your monthly expenses, but it is important to understand that to live costs money, which requires some kind of regular income.

One of the biggest shocks for young people is the realization that just about everything costs money. When Mom and Dad are looking after things, lifestyle costs don't enter your mind. The earlier you experience the connection between daily buying decisions and their costs the better. If you do, you'll be better equipped for the real world, on your own. The more prepared you are for independent living ahead of time, the easier the transition will be.

A young client of mine recalled how his first few months of independent living had gone when he was just 18. With his own apartment and some distance from his parents, he could taste his new sense of freedom. After just one month of bills had built up, he suddenly realized he didn't have sufficient funds to pay them. He was soon living back at home again, having learned a valuable lesson. Living expenses are a fact of life and we have to manage our money and income so that we can handle the bills that will inevitably come our way.

3

What Is a Mortgage and How Does It Work?

Let's say you loaned a friend some money and you told her she had to pay you back the original amount plus interest (extra money) over a period of years. That, in essence, would be a mortgage: an amount of money borrowed generally to buy a home. It is an agreement between a lender (usually a bank or trust company) and a client (the person borrowing the money). The borrower agrees to pay back the borrowed money plus interest, usually over a period of years.

Here are some words commonly used when talking about mortgages:

- **Principal** – the original amount of money borrowed;
- **Amortization period** – the period of time (usually years) over which the payback period applies (payback of both principal and interest);
- **Interest** – the additional money (quoted in percentage rates of return) to be paid, in addition to the original principal amount;
- **Pre-payment** – term that refers to the ability to pay a portion (often up to 10% of the principal) each year in addition to regular monthly payments of both principal and interest;
- **Open mortgage** – suggests full flexibility to pay mortgage off or make changes to the terms without penalties or extra fees;
- **Closed mortgage** – suggests that mortgage terms and conditions are fixed and unchangeable for the timeframe in question (1 year, 3 years, 5 years or whatever).

The majority of homeowners acquire their properties with the use of a mortgage, mainly because the price is too high to pay in cash. After all, homes are among the biggest investments most people make in their lifetimes. Mortgages are becoming more flexible in terms of pay-back privileges and in taking advantage of lower interest rates.

It may be easier to think of a mortgage as a big bill that typically takes many years longer to pay off compared to most other bills. I've had clients tell me that taking on large debt like a mortgage is an intimidating experience but when you break it down, it is much like other bills or debts that have a principal component and interest. For home ownership and other purposes, mortgages are useful and valuable instruments to have working for you.

4

What Is a Good Interest Rate?

Before answering this question, we should explain that money we make on investments comes in different forms. You receive interest from a savings account, bonds or a guaranteed investment certificate. You receive interest or dividend income or capital gains when you invest in companies and businesses (stocks or equities).

History tells us that each of these investments (or asset classes) have delivered different average rates of return over time. A broad mix of equity-based investments (stocks) have typically generated higher average rates of return compared to cash and fixed-income interest-bearing alternatives (bonds and GICs). So how hard the investment works to build capital or how productive it is, is relevant as we consider good interest rates.

Another factor is the effect of taxes, because interest income is 100% taxable, whereas dividends and capital gains are taxed at a lesser rate. And while this may not be a big issue when your income and marginal tax rate are low, it will become a larger issue as your tax rate increases with increased levels of income.

So what is a good interest rate? The answer really depends on your goals, expectations and timeframe. A GIC paying 5% per year for five years is clearly better than a savings account paying 2%. However, if you need access to your money before the GIC maturity date (as it may be non-redeemable), it's no longer a better investment because the money isn't available when you need it.

History shows that equities (stocks) would most likely deliver greater growth than the other investment classes over a multi-year timeframe. But if you need the money a year after investing (even though your original time horizon was multi-year) and your investments are worth less than when you began, due to poor market conditions, then equities will have proven to be the wrong choice.

A good interest rate or, better still, a good investment is one that meets your needs, expectations and your timeframe. Interest rates or returns are a factor but only one among many as you can see.

It is quite common for me to hear a client express their frustration over their lack of gains, after taxes have been paid, on a GIC or savings account. While the investment may have been guaranteed to go up each year, the reality was quite different, once taxes were paid on those meager gains. It is important to understand the implications of your investment choices, returns being just one among many variables to consider.

5

How Do I Figure Out
How Much Income I Need?

I like this question because it goes against the natural flow of things. Here's what I mean.

Most of us start a job or career once high school and possibly college and university are complete. One job follows another without any real planning involved. It's rare to run into someone who planned exactly what they were going to do with their career and did it. The reason for this is that life introduces many unpredictable variables, any one of which may influence or change your plan for work or career.

Most of us adjust our lifestyle to the income our job or career gives us. If we don't do that; everything soon falls apart. You can't spend $3,000 per month for any length of time, when your income is half that.

A client by the name of Sarah told me that in one year she moved three times and changed jobs twice, before she finally learned the connection between income and lifestyle expenses. Initially, she found lifestyle expenses exceeded her income, necessitating changes. When she cut her living costs (by moving into a less expensive home) and increased her income (by changing jobs), she could afford the lifestyle she was seeking. This was a vital life lesson to learn after one year chalk full of change.

A useful exercise to go through is to discuss how much it costs each year to live in your current lifestyle. Ask your parents how much it costs them for a year's worth of living. Write down the main cost components. After that, figure our how much income you'd need to cover these costs. Ask yourself if that's the lifestyle you seek, or do you want more.

This exercise gives you a frame of reference. It's a great starting point. If you want a bigger home, nicer car, etc., estimate how much higher your income would have to be to afford these added costs. Your desired income must link with two important factors, namely, education/training and your preferred career or job.

If your parents, teachers or friends can't help you with this exercise, then approach a financial planner or investment advisor. They are trained to assist with these sorts of issues. The key here is to begin to think about the lifestyle you want and the income you'll need.

A few closing comments about this topic:

- Your income, or how much money you need or want, is just one dimension among many in life. Be mindful of the old adage that says money or income never made anyone happy. You will be far better off in life choosing a job or career that you love but pays you less, than a career that pays well but makes you miserable. Be aware, as well, that today's generation will often experience several jobs or careers over a working lifetime. Developing skills that are transferable and useful in a variety of areas makes you more broadly marketable for different jobs/careers.

- Building wealth has nothing to do with how much you make. It has far more to do with what 'you do' with the income you make. In other words, if you make wise investment decisions with a lower income, you may well build more capital than the higher paid person who is less disciplined with their money. Establishing some sort of budget that lists estimated living costs is a good starting point. Use your parents' living expenses and income as a frame of reference. After all, that's how you're living today.

- Interview people with careers and income levels that match your own aspirations. You'll find that in most cases, your chosen interviewees will be happy to share their life experiences with you.

This process will give you insight into the career you are considering, and the income you might earn from it.

6

What Does It Mean to Have Financial Security?

Any two people will define 'financial security' differently, but there are some common understandings of this term.

Generally, people think of having enough money or capital to see them through uncertain times in their lives and throughout their retirement years – that stage of life where most of us are no longer earning an income.

To be financially secure means having enough money to cover your lifestyle expenses (or those of your loved ones) if you become disabled, become unemployed, when you retire and when you die.

All of this requires planning and important decisions at various points throughout your life. Things are less complex when you're single and become more involved if you get married and have children.

Money from investments and insurance products provides the basis for this financial security. Money, to maintain your lifestyle, must come from somewhere (if not your job) and unless you win lotteries or inherit money, these are the logical sources.

But the real benefit of financial security is peace of mind. If you're investing wisely and doing smart things with your money, you have the pleasure of focussing more time and energy on life's real priorities: your loved ones, your career, your hobbies and other interests.

Eric, a client in his twenties, reflected on the importance of financial security. He'd seen his parents struggle all their lives due to lack of money, only because they had never made building financial security a priority. He was determined to avoid such an insecure fate. As a result, his commitment to an investment program with appropriate insurance protection was his number one goal.

Sometimes we imagine living a life without frustration, fear, anger and challenges to overcome. The reality is that each of us will face difficulties in our lives.

Adversity deepens our resolve and makes us stronger. When it comes to building financial security, it's better to get money working 'for us' rather than the other way around. With some advance planning, money management doesn't have to be one of your major challenges. You'll have your hands full and life will be more than interesting enough with all the other challenges.

Finally, financial security is not really a destination. It's an active process, a mindset that is lifelong. Making wise decisions with money and investments starts when you're a teen, and the benefits extend to loved ones beyond your lifetime.

If the idea of building financial security is appealing, begin the dialogue with family members and professionals and start taking the steps to achieve it.

7

How Do You Invest?

Before answering how to invest, perhaps it helps to consider the meaning of the word 'invest'.

Do you remember the first time you took your allowance to the bank? Instead of spending your money on a toy or gum or candy, you were introduced to the notion of saving and investing. Saving may involve keeping your earnings in a piggy bank or growing interest income in an actual bank account. Most of us start out saving our money by putting it in a bank savings account. As we get older, we become aware of other ways to grow our money other than in these conventional accounts.

Investing generally implies getting our money working in better ways than a savings or chequing account can deliver. There are many different investments or vehicles where your money may be more productive (earn more money), namely, stocks, bonds, GICs (guaranteed investment certificates), real estate and mutual funds, to name just a few. I'll say more on these investments in another chapter.

Now, back to how we invest. Today there are many ways to invest your money. You can meet with various investment professionals and benefit from their advice; you can go to the local bank to invest; or you can set up an investment account over the Internet. All methods give you the option of investing a certain amount each month or a specific lump sum amount, once you've signed appropriate papers and established an account.

You may instruct the financial institution, bank, trust company, investment dealer or mutual fund company to take your desired investment amounts out of your chequing account automatically (which is the easiest way) or you may personally deliver or mail investments as you like.

I had a client tell me that she didn't invest over a ten year period, from age 20 to 30 for one reason; she didn't know how to invest. "I was intimidated by anything to do with money and investing and avoided the subject just because I was afraid to ask questions and appear stupid."

This may sound strange but it is all too common. Never hesitate to ask questions and learn from others about their experiences. You'll be glad you did.

Perhaps the more important things you need to decide are how much to invest, the timeframe involved and the purpose of your investment. And whom do you trust with your investments if you decide not to go it alone? We'll look at these topics separately in the following pages.

8

How Much Should I Invest Per Month?

This question relates to two different points.

What percentage of your money do you need to invest per month?

That depends on several things. If you're living at home and you don't have to pay for clothes, lodging or food, then you can contribute most of your income from a job, allowances, and gifts to your investment plan.

If you have a lot of expenses, you may not have much left over to invest. It's a good idea to pay yourself first by investing for your benefit every month if you can. If at all possible, treat the 'pay yourself first' expense as your first priority.

Your short, medium and longterm goals will determine how much you 'need' to invest per month. If you're saving for a stereo system for example, figure out the cost and how much you'll need to save or invest. That's an example of a short-term goal. If however, it is more important for you to have a million dollars by the time you're 40, then you need to invest what this requires, assuming certain average rates of return.

Using historical experience as our guide, we can estimate average rates of return (within a range) on our investments. We've learned that investing in savings or chequing accounts will likely be less productive compared to guaranteed investment certificates or bonds. We also know that owning shares of companies and businesses (equities) will likely build more money than GICs or bonds, over the longterm. At the same time, risk of short-term drops or loss increases with more productive investments. Risk and reward go hand in hand. Over time, the risk of losing money associated with equities is reduced thanks to compounding growth (a term which simply means growth on top of an ever expanding base).

So, relating to our original question, the percentage of income (money) you need to invest per month depends upon your goals (short, medium and longterm) and the timeframe to achieve those goals. It also depends on your priorities and how much personal spending you're willing to sacrifice.

A teenager named Scott seemed to struggle with this idea of how much to invest. He couldn't get his mind around a number and couldn't seem to get started. We decided to start out small with an amount of $50 per month, and grow from there if he could afford it. After a few months, he said he never even noticed that there was less money in his bank account and proceeded to double his monthly investment. A few months after that, he doubled it again. In Scott's case, he just needed to get started–it was easy going after that.

What percentage of income or growth might you expect from your investments?

As mentioned earlier, the rate of return or 'ROR' is really how much you're able to grow your money over a period of time. Where short periods of time are concerned, say three years or less, you may be able to make a considerable amount of money by investing in companies or businesses (equities) but you may also lose thanks to the day to day up and down unpredictable movement of stock markets. Savings accounts, GICs and bonds are a less productive but more secure place to invest your money, especially if the timeframe is short. For longer timeframes, you're more likely to experience greater growth by investing in the more productive asset class, namely equities (ideally a diversified mix of companies in a variety of industries).

Yes, equities will always vary in value thanks to ever changing market conditions. However, over longer timeframes, equities have typically delivered higher average rates of return compared to more conservative investments.

9

Which Fund Company Is the Most Productive?

It's helpful to establish an understanding of investment or mutual funds before addressing this question:

What Are Investment or Mutual Funds?

Today, investing in mutual funds is probably the most popular means of investing for Canadians. When you invest in these funds, you're really hiring professional money managers who have expertise in building investment portfolios, according to a specific mandate or guiding philosophy. An example of this would be a fund whose managers specialize in investing in Canadian companies or stocks (otherwise known as equities). You're putting your trust in the talent and experience of your chosen team (fund) along with thousands of other investors. Many investors use financial planners or investment advisors to choose which teams (funds) are most suitable, and for those that don't, there is always the Internet.

Let's return to our main question. Which fund company is the most productive? If there were one fund or stock or investment that was more productive or performed better than all others, then any rational person would own it. Of course, some funds, stocks or specific investments have performed better than others over given periods, but beyond that general statement, there are many factors that make absolute answers impossible.

It's not unlike asking who is the most productive baseball or hockey player. There are many categories and factors you have to consider. For example, who was the superior hockey player among Jaromir Jagr, Joe Sakic, Mario Lemieux and Wayne Gretzky? Which year do you pick as you attempt to answer such a question? How do you compare different styles/positions? There are so many variables at play.

A fund may have been very productive with superior investment results over the previous year, but may not have done as well over a three-year period. Another fund may have dropped less in value in tough market conditions compared to a more volatile fund, yet the latter fund may have a higher average return. Some would consider dropping less in value in negative market conditions, as more important than higher returns. There are many different kinds of investment funds with different purposes or mandates.

While investment performance is always an important factor, there are many others to think about in the process of deciding what teams or funds are most suitable for your goals, timeframe and comfort zone. Establishing that all-important link between your interests and an investment product or strategy is key, and that link is what industry professionals (planners and advisors) are trained to address.

10

How Do You Invest In a Stock?

It is possible to invest in stocks in a variety of ways. Here's a sample of the most obvious ones.

Stockbrokers/Investment Advisors

Investors seeking advice on the buying/selling of companies often work with stock brokerage firms and/or banks that offer a range of services. The investor typically pays the broker a commission for each transaction or on an annual fee basis. Recommendations to buy or sell a company are made by the broker/advisor drawing on research provided by analysts who are fellow staff within the organization.

Discount brokers/Financial Planners

It is possible to buy/sell stocks once an account is set-up using the services of a discount broker either by phone or the internet. Discount brokers and some financial planners will process the transaction without offering advice. The idea here is to provide a simple, no-advice transactional service for the investor who already knows what he wants to buy/sell. For this reduced service, there is typically a lower fee structure.

With any professional you may work with in the financial services industry, it is important that you feel you can relate to them and that your investment objectives are 'in line' with their working philosophy. Once a relationship and a guiding investment philosophy are established, the process of buying and selling stocks or any other investments may begin.

The Internet has revolutionized the way we do many things. There are positive and negative aspects to any topic we care to debate and the use of the Internet for investment purposes is no exception. The fact that we can open accounts and use our computers to buy/sell stocks (or any other investments) is a great tool for some and a recipe for disaster for others. For those with the interest, experience, expertise, patience and discipline, Internet or phone based investment decisions may be entirely appropriate. Still, for most investors, the benefits of a relationship with a trusted planner/advisor outweigh the convenience of operating alone.

Several of my clients have recounted that at one time they were serious stock buyers, but that they eventually tended toward professionally managed mutual funds and other similarly managed portfolios. When I asked why, their answer was always the same. They found it frustrating to have to watch the day to day movement of stocks and try to time their buying and selling. It was too often an unsuccessful process and the stress burden was too much. Discovering what form of investing is best for you is an important early step as you build for the future.

11

How Do I Tell Which Companies I Want to Invest in and Whether or Not Certain Companies Will Do Well?

If you're going to buy stocks or equity mutual funds on your own, it helps to have the interest, expertise and time to make these decisions. If you were missing any one of these variables, you would be wise to consult a financial professional before investing. And even if you have these variables intact, an experienced and rational professional can add a great deal of value to your life.

One of the most difficult concepts for new investors to appreciate is that it is possible for a fund, stock or portfolio to struggle, even lose money over defined periods but also rebuild into a respectable investment over time. This is where experience and patience are invaluable. Some times it pays to hold on to an investment over the long term even if it declines in value in the short term.

There are many variables brokers and analysts use to assess whether or not to invest in a company and, therefore, to determine which ones have good prospects. A good history related to earnings, cash flow, debt levels, profitability, quality of management, core product focus and an unwavering commitment to their vision, represent just a few of the many variables they consider.

There are various courses you can take that will help you understand more about stock markets and investing in general. Your local community colleges offer courses, the Canadian Securities Institute offers a full list of courses, and many others are available through associations related to financial planning. There's always the library or your local bookstore where you'll find a variety of books on investing. Or, you might subscribe to investment magazines or 'surf the net' for evaluations of companies or stocks of interest. There are programs on TV and radio as well, which might help you along.

There is really no magic way of knowing which companies will do well. You could sit in a room with several investment 'experts', each with years of success at investing, and find them disagreeing about the merits of owning a particular company.

Investing successfully on a consistent basis over a long period of time is very hard to do, even for some of the best investment minds in the world.

There is a world-famous investor by the name of Warren Buffet whose stock picks at certain times looked like they didn't make sense. If you look at certain timeframes, some of his individual holdings (stock picks) may not have turned out well at all. Over the long haul (meaning decades in his case) however, Buffet's 'buy familiar quality companies and hold them for the long term' philosophy has given him a remarkable record of achievement.

Picking 'hot' companies or investing in the 'right' companies requires knowledge, discipline and patience, and even then, there are no guarantees you'll invest successfully. It would be wrong to say you couldn't succeed on your own. However, most people see their limitations and invest using the expertise of investment professionals who make mistakes, but who generally win more often than they lose.

12

When Is the Appropriate Time to Invest in Stocks?

On the surface, this seems to be a simple question that deserves a simple answer. The complexity of it may become clear in the example below, where we'll refer to a hypothetical company X.

During the higher point in the market in the last few years, company X was trading in the stock market at over $120 per share. At that point, many market analysts, stockbrokers and industry observers were suggesting that investing in company X, along with many other companies, was a good idea as still better times and improving market values were ahead.

It is impossible to be wrong with the benefit of hindsight, and we know that only months after these predictions, the value of company X and many other companies plummeted, due to a deep and prolonged negative (bear) market. This drop was even more substantial due to the impact of three consecutive poor (bear) markets.

According to some brokers, analysts and industry observers, company X was a recommended 'buy' even when it was worth over $100 per share, though many at the time were suggesting the company and the industry generally were over-valued (stocks were selling for more than they were worth).

Was it appropriate to buy company X at over $100 per share? Perhaps it was if you held it to the point where it was $120 and sold. In this scenario, you would have made money. But it would not have been profitable if you had bought it at $100 and sold it when it was worth substantially less. It seems the concept of buying a stock at an 'appropriate' time is more complicated than it might seem.

This is really the heart of the issue. A stock purchase that is appropriate for one broker, analyst, investment observer or regular investor may be inappropriate for another. There are many variables involved in determining whether a stock is appropriate to own.

Regular investors and professionals have different philosophies, timeframes, investment styles and comfort zones on top of specific variables that include earnings, cash flow, profitability, etc., that analysts often study. We can see this point more clearly by looking just at timeframe. Buying company X at $100 may make sense if the holding period is multi-year (say 10 years or longer), on the assumption the company has a good longterm outlook. Buying company X at $100 with a three-year timeframe might work, but could also prove disastrous in the event it declines, and you need your money in that short a timeframe.

Depending upon the investment criteria used by a broker, analyst or professional manager, you'll often get different, even conflicting responses, as to the wisdom of buying a particular stock at a specific point in time. So, what seems quite simple is in actual fact quite a complex matter when you factor in all the considerations. And the complexity only increases when you add to the equation the issue of holding period - or when to sell.

Whether or not you are the type of person that should be buying individual stocks must be addressed first. There are seasoned brokers/investors who have been investing for decades who now refuse to buy/sell stocks on their own, even though they may have done so actively in the past. They have moved to professional management, where teams with particular experience and expertise make investment decisions on their behalf.

Penny is a living example of such a decision. She considered herself an experienced investor in both mutual funds and individual stocks. But even though her investment choices turned out well most of the time, she always felt stress about when to buy and sell. In time, she decided her best move was to let a portfolio management team make those decisions for her, operating on the advice of a financial advisor. So she moved her money into a recommended portfolio and no longer carried the burden and stress of timing (and other) decisions respecting her investments. Years later, she has never regretted that move.

There are those individuals who prefer to operate on their own and want to decide the suitability of investing in a particular stock. No matter how you look at this, there are many important variables to consider, each one of which should be carefully assessed.

13

Can My Investments
Go Down in Value?

This question gets to the heart of a very important consideration in the world of investing. Most teens have only experienced owning a bank savings account. As a result, they have only seen the value of their account go up over the years, or at least that's what they perceive when they look at their bankbooks or statements.

A term you may have heard before is "inflation". Simply put, it represents the gradual increase in the cost of goods and services over time. An example of this is to compare the cost of ordinary items like milk or bread years ago with today's prices. I bring inflation up because if prices go up on average more than what we earn in a bank savings account, then we are actually losing money. If inflation averages 3% per year and your bank account gives you 1% per year, then you're losing an average of 2% per year on your money. Put another way, a single loonie today would buy you less than what a dollar bought you one, two or three years ago. The reality of inflation is that prices go up each year for the things we buy every day to live. Decades ago, it used to cost two cents to send a letter; it now costs 51 cents to send the same letter. Another way to think of the effect of increasing prices for goods and services would be to picture a one-dollar paper bill (assuming one existed today). Take scissors and cut off a bit of that bill every year and imagine yourself trying to buy the same item as the year before – it won't work because the one-dollar bill is worth less. Over the last 40 years or so, inflation has actually averaged closer to 5% per year, even more than the example used here.

So if inflation is more than what you earn in your bank savings account, then the value of your account or investment actually goes down in value; something that may seem impossible but in actual fact is entirely true. But, that's not all. Then there is the tax impact. As your income goes up, the more tax you pay, and because 100% of interest income from bank savings accounts is taxable, there may be even less in your pocket that's yours after inflation and taxes have taken their toll. Using the example above, you would indeed be losing money every year even if you paid no taxes. With tax payments, the loss would be even greater.

What then is the point of mentioning the impact of inflation and taxes considering our central question – "can my investments go down in value?"

For many Canadians, supposedly safe and secure bank savings accounts, guaranteed investment certificates (GICs) and bonds are the way to build financial security. There are two implications that come to mind with this approach. These same people may not be growing money (building capital) at all, when you factor in the ravaging effects of inflation and taxes. Using another example, if your GIC pays 5% and inflation is 3% and you pay the other 2% back in taxes, you're not actually gaining ground at all. The 5% gain is offset by the loss of value due to inflation and taxes.

During bear or poor markets, where investments in companies and businesses (stocks or equity-based mutual funds) haven't done as well, bank savings accounts, GICs or bonds may seem attractive. However over the longterm, typically a decade or more, these conservative investments will not likely build capital, particularly after taxes and inflation, nearly as well as a diversified pool of equities.

Individual companies can go bankrupt and lose all of their value. Companies do drop in value during individual years or over periods of years, as was witnessed recently in the bear market of 2000-2003. For investors with short timeframes, typically five years or less, equities may not be appropriate, but over ten years or longer, history has generally favoured the investor that has been invested in a diversified pool of equities. In other words, over short periods, equities are unpredictable and may lose money, yet over long periods, an investor has a greater chance of making money compared to most other investment strategies.

Individual companies or groups of companies (equities) do go down in value from time to time. They also grow in value, on average noticeably more than savings accounts, GICs and bonds over longer timeframes. Savings accounts, GICs and bonds also make money if they grow more than the cost of inflation and taxes. The key to this question is not what happens during any given year (unless you need your money for that year) but what happens to your money over the long haul (defined here as ten years or longer). It is the average rate of return that really matters. You may experience three negative years out of 10 but still have a positive average that is markedly higher than savings accounts, GICs and bonds could deliver after inflation and taxes. What happens over a specific year shouldn't matter over the long term – it's the 'average' rate of return that matters. Here's what I mean using hypothetical, yet realistic compounding growth estimates:

- $1,000 invested in a savings account averaging 3% is worth $1,806 after 20 years;
- $1,000 invested in a GIC averaging 4% is worth $2,191 after 20 years;
- $1,000 invested in a bond averaging 5% is worth $2,653 after 20 years;
- $1,000 invested in a group of stocks (equities) averaging 8% is worth $4,661 after 20 years.

Another way to consider inevitable drops in value is to look at the following table. Assume investment #1 is a GIC guaranteeing 4% per year for 10 years, thus delivering a 4% average rate of return over the 10-year period. Investment #2 has both negative and positive numbers in it. Think of these numbers as the actual returns (gains or losses) experienced in the given years.

	Yr 1	*Yr 2*	*Yr 3*	*Yr 4*	*Yr 5*
#1	4%	4%	4%	4%	4%
#2	10%	15%	-3%	-7%	-5%

	Yr 6	*Yr 7*	*Yr 8*	*Yr 9*	*Yr 10*
#1	4%	4%	4%	4%	4%
#2	17%	19%	13%	-6%	14%

Average Return

#1   4%

#2   6.7%

While most of us would naturally prefer to experience only growth with our investments, we may be missing out on greater growth, particularly after inflation and taxes have taken their toll, by not being prepared to live with greater fluctuation or volatility. Few of us would like to live with three negative years in a row (years three, four and five), as in #2 above, yet the average rate of return over 10 years is more than 50% more than investment #1 delivered. If you had started out with $1,000, investment #1 would give you $1,480, whereas investment #2 would deliver $1,913 ($433 more) ten years later.

Knowing the implications of the two investment strategies, which investment would you prefer now? If you need your money in five years or less, investment #2 would not be the best choice given that years three, four and five were negative. On the other hand, if you have a longterm timeframe for your money and feel comfortable with the concept of negative individual years with equities, then you may be better suited for the second strategy. Finally, factoring the ravaging effects of inflation and taxes into the equation, which literally eat away at the value of your money, you quickly appreciate that it is important to be concerned about growth, especially over longer timeframes. The cost of doing otherwise may be great indeed.

14

If I Choose To Work With A Professional, Which One Should It Be?

In the investment/financial planning world, there are different kinds of professionals who have expertise to offer the public. Broadly speaking, there are financial planners and investment advisors, some of whom have special industry designations or professional credentials. Just as there are teachers and employers you like to work with and others you don't, the same holds true for financial planners and brokers. Beyond their professional credentials, there are important factors including their personality, experience, age/stage of life, personal chemistry and level of service.

If your parents or friends are working with someone they like, then that personal endorsement is valuable. You may want to work with someone who is trusted by family or friends. If your family or friends don't know a planner or advisor, you may want to ask your accountant or lawyer for a reference. Often these professionals have networks of their own which include financial planners and investment advisors. Finally, if none of the above are options, simply set-up an appointment with several planners or advisors to see if they work with people in your circumstances. You'll want to be as comfortable as possible with the planner or advisor you pick.

In the interview process, ask them how they invest themselves. This may give you an idea of their natural bias toward one style of investing versus another. Ask about their experience and professional credentials. Ask about frequency of contact and level of service so that you're clear about expectations. Ask to speak to existing clients and ask them about their experience to-date with their planner/advisor. Once you've chosen someone, make a commitment to yourself to work with your planner/advisor and stay in touch with him or her. He or she will only be as useful as you choose to make them. Let me give you an example of my own personal experience in this regard.

When I began investing, my financial planner was someone I had rapport with right away. I knew I could trust him – I felt his integrity. He wanted to help me reach my goals. He was also a man with a broad client base and was very busy. I didn't wait for him to call, send an e-mail or mail me a letter in order for us to communicate. He wasn't in touch with me every week, month, quarter or even necessarily every year, except by mail. I knew however, that I could trust him and felt comfortable enough to call him and chat or arrange for an appointment at any time. I didn't get upset if he didn't call at regular intervals. I knew he was busy, but I also knew that his busy calendar would not stop us from connecting if we needed to.

My message here is that it's up to you to stay in touch with your planner/broker. If you're looking for that professional to add value to your life, then take the initiative to stay in touch with him or her. You'll be glad you did. To borrow a famous phrase from President John F. Kennedy, "Ask not what your country can do for you but what you can do for your country". In this instance, this famous phrase could be changed to, "the success of the relationship with your planner depends not on the contact they make with you but rather on the initiative and effort you put into the relationship". I don't expect my doctor or lawyer or accountant or mechanic to call me, but if I need them, I'm well advised to make the effort to stay in touch and get the most out of the relationship. Successful relationships always need to be maintained from both sides, not just from one side. The expression, 'you get what you pay for' applies here where we benefit, when we invest in relationships in terms of time, energy, money or all of the above. This advice applies to all relationships we assume in life.

15

What Is a Loan
(& Related Questions)?

At its simplest level, a loan is nothing more than a promise to pay back money you borrow. There are a few other factors involved if and when you get a loan from financial institutions. Here are the main ones.

There are many reasons you may need to borrow money throughout your lifetime: to finance your education, buy a car, buy furniture, buy a home, pay for a wedding, and the list goes on. Anytime you're borrowing money, you're getting a loan.

Where banks or trust companies or other financial

organizations are involved, you commit or promise to pay the loan back over a certain period of time (usually monthly) at a certain interest rate or additional cost. There must be some financial advantage for the lending party to loan you the money in the first place and that financial benefit is the interest rate. You pay them money on top of the loaned amount that you must repay.

As we've said, there is no shortage of things that you might like to acquire or own during your teen years, let alone the rest of your life. We need to be cautious about loans for two main reasons. Taking a loan really means taking on debt. If debt gets out of hand, it may lead to loss of control and confidence. And while there are useful and helpful forms of debt, it is important not to forget that there is a downside to debt, if it is not managed responsibly.

It is wise to establish a list of things you want to buy, set priorities for those items and set aside your own money to acquire them. Paying high interest rate charges after using your credit card means you're paying more for something than if you'd saved the money and paid for it yourself. It takes discipline and patience to acquire things on your own, but you'll appreciate it more if you do it that way and you won't have the problem of a growing debt load that you may not be able to pay off.

Most of us get loans for university or college, a car

and to finance the purchase of a home (this debt is called a mortgage). But not all loans are created equal. Some carry high interest-rate charges (like credit cards) and may be inflexible with respect to payback terms and conditions. It's very important that you think carefully about what you're trying to accomplish and live within your means. Life is complicated enough without adding an unnecessary financial burden.

What Do You Require to Get a Loan?

Most lending institutions require evidence of income and a good credit history. The income relates to your ability to pay back the loan plus interest. A good credit history means that you have a history of paying your debts on a timely basis. By checking the information available on your social insurance number (SIN #), the lending institution is able to determine what kind of history you've established regarding payment of previous debts.

Often, where income isn't high enough and where no credit history exists, young people sometimes involve their parent in the transaction as co-signer. This way, the income and credit history requirements may be met with a parent involved.

It is to your advantage to learn to manage income as early as possible, in order to develop a good credit history. Lending institutions are more likely to look favourably at a young applicant who has taken on jobs and managed money and debt responsibly. The sooner you do this, the less dependent you become on others. It is another mark of adulthood and moving forward in a positive and mature manner.

How Do You Take Out a Loan?

The process of taking out a loan is quite simple. You either visit a bank or trust company or other lending institution in person, by phone or over the Internet. Some loans require face-to-face meetings, and others don't. As mentioned, some institutions require a co-signer, when income or credit history is missing or insufficient.

In every case, information is exchanged about the purpose and timeframe of the loan and your personal ability to make payments. Whether or not the loan makes sense for you to pursue is the real issue – one you should discuss with parents, trusted friends and/or a financial professional.

How Long Do You Have to Pay Back a Loan?

The length of time you have to pay back a loan is different for every loan you take. Big-ticket items, such as homes and cars, often take years to repay, whereas paying for clothes that you might put onto a credit card are typically paid back over a period of months. The interest charged on credit cards is higher than almost any other loan so it is important to pay credit card debt immediately, so as to reduce unnecessary interest costs.

It's important to consider your cash flow (how much you earn) and your ability to consistently make the payments. Life can be frustrating if you take on debt and struggle everyday to make the payments. It may be an added burden that you don't need in your life. On the other hand, loans are part of most people's lives, and as long as you can handle the payments, it may be your best strategy to achieve your goal.

I have clients who fall into opposite categories where loans and debt are concerned. Some are quite content to carry expensive loans, year to year, for a lifetime and it doesn't bother them a bit. That's simply their personality and they understand the link between the debt and their purpose for it. Others can't sleep at night living with debt and would do anything in their power to avoid it altogether. It always helps to know yourself, to seek different opinions and be as rational as you can when entertaining loans and debt. There are many worthy goals achieved using loans and carrying debt. You just have to decide, with the help of professionals, whether your goals are best satisfied in this manner.

16

What Is an RRSP?

RRSPs refer to Registered Retirement Savings Plans that you hear your parents and the media talking about all the time. Anything that is registered usually means the government is behind the initiative. Let me explain.

Years ago, the federal government thought it wise to motivate Canadians to begin investing for their future retirement needs. We don't need to get into why they felt this made sense, but logic would suggest there were concerns that the Canada Pension Plan and Old Age Security may not provide enough income after retirement. These are other government-supported programs geared toward assisting Canadians with their cost of living in the final stages of their lives, typically during retirement.

An RRSP isn't a specific investment like a bond or a mutual fund, though RRSPs may contain these individual products. It's a plan registered with the federal government where the investments inside it are tax deductible (in the year of contribution) and designated for retirement purposes. The investments inside an RRSP are tax sheltered (in other words, free from any tax liability) until such time as they are redeemed, at which point they are 100% taxable.

RRSPs have certain rules, like most government programs. One is that you have to be earning an income, since the amount of money you may contribute is determined by a percentage (18 percent) of the previous year's earned income. Secondly, the investments you put into your RRSP plan must be RRSP eligible (meeting investment definition guidelines as determined by the federal government).

Investments that qualify as RRSP eligible include any of the following:

- savings accounts
- treasury bills
- GICs
- bonds

- mutual funds
- stocks
- and more (this is not a complete list)

So an RRSP is like a basket that holds any number of investments that meet the RRSP eligible guidelines.

One day my client Jim said he wanted to buy an RRSP. I then asked him what particular investment he wanted within his RRSP. He looked confused and said again that he wanted an RRSP. I explained that there are many types of investments that we could consider for his RRSP. After further clarification, Jim realized we needed to be specific about the nature of his preferred investment, to be sure it was suitable for his goals, risk tolerance and timeframe. The term RRSP is generic and doesn't refer to a specific investment at all. This is worth remembering as you consider RRSP investments.

17

How Do You
Start Saving for RRSPs?

In essence, you simply need to review how much money you can afford to invest on a monthly or lump sum basis and then arrange to invest that money. But let's break this question down to be sure we don't miss anything.

We've dealt with the 'how' in earlier chapters. To summarize, you visit your financial planner, bank or investment advisor and make arrangements to deposit money on a monthly or lump sum basis. Or, if you're using an internet method, you would arrange to have money transferred from say a chequing account to an investment account and proceed from there.

How do you 'start' to invest? By doing the above, namely the 'how', you'll have begun. But starting to invest (while good on its own) has more meaning and purpose if linked to a goal.

It is interesting to know that if you invest $20 per month (for example) starting at age 13, you'll have $928,884 at age 75 if you earn an average rate of return of 10%. And, all you would have invested is $14,880 over those 62 years!

We know from studying human behaviour, that students who set goals, athletes who aim for records to achieve, and business people with targets to exceed, typically do better than those who don't set goals. By knowing what it takes to achieve certain goals, including financial security (having enough money for life), you may be more likely to do what the goal requires and to ultimately succeed.

Saving is a good idea for lots of reasons, but investing may be even more helpful. Saving relates more to putting money aside, say in a bank savings account, for short term needs, including a vacation, taxes, gifts, credit card expenses and other regular bills. Saving for these short-term needs demands stable and non-fluctuating investments so the money will be there to pay for the vacation, credit card bills, etc.

Registered Retirement Savings Plans (known as RRSPs) generally don't relate to short-term needs. Most of us put money aside in registered plans in order to have enough money to live comfortably when we're retired and no longer earning an income. This is the main purpose of retirement savings plans, as the name implies.

We now turn our attention back to saving versus investing.

Investing relates more to building enough money for our future needs. And since RRSPs are the main vehicle that Canadians use to build capital (money), we need to make sure the vehicles we choose to invest in will deliver the capital our retirement demands.

Productive investments include equity-based vehicles (stocks, equity mutual funds). Of course, there are bonds, GICs and cash vehicles, but history has shown these instruments do not build capital as successfully over the long term. So it's important to look carefully at the investment vehicles to be sure you have the potential of building enough capital to secure a comfortable retirement.

While RRSPs are a well-known investment vehicle for your future retirement needs, it is not the only nor is it necessarily the best way to invest for your future. We'll discuss this idea further in another chapter.

Investing in RRSPs for your future well-being begins as soon as money becomes available. Whether it's allowance, gifts of cash from grandparents or earned income from a job, the key is to begin to invest. You can't begin too early; just get started and the benefits will flow. Starting early is key because time is your greatest ally in your efforts to build enough capital for your future needs.

Investing in non-registered vehicles (non-RRSPs) or regular, open investments with your advisor, planner, bank or via the 'net', may be done at any time. Unlike RRSPs, which have special rules to follow, 'open' or non-registered investing offers the greatest flexibility.

One of the most common investment strategies for younger people is 'in trust for' investment accounts usually set up by parents or grandparents. The idea is for the parent or grandparent to retain control of the account until the age of majority is reached, at which point the child becomes fully in control of the money.

When in doubt about saving and investing, just get started, "just do it" as the Nike commercials say. If you've found you're investing too much, then reduce the amount appropriately. If you can afford more, then increase your monthly or lump sum contribution. By getting started, you'll overcome the biggest hurdle for most of us- inaction. When investing, time is a great ally and you need to use it for your benefit.

18

What is an RESP?

Just as the government has offered special incentives for those who invest in Registered Retirement Savings Plans, they have done the same for those who invest in Registered Educational Savings Plans for children.

RESPs have two special features: 1) the investments (money) are tax sheltered until such time as the money is redeemed, and 2) there is grant money given by the government up to certain limits, $400 maximum per year per individual (20% of $2000 contribution) which provides an added bonus or incentive for parents to invest with their children's future education needs in mind. So, for every contribution every year (with some restrictions), you have the added benefit of free grant money to add to your own RESP investments.

RESP plans have other special features which distinguish them from other regular open investments. Without getting into all the details, here are the main ones:

- the investment contributions, capital growth and grant money are intended for individual or family use;
- once the money is in the hands of the beneficiary, the capital growth and grant are taxable whereas the principal contribution is not;
- if the money is not used by the beneficiary, the capital growth may be moved to the subscriber's RRSP if the subscriber has RRSP room in the year of the withdrawal;

While RESPs have become quite popular, thanks in particular to the free grant money, there are other ways to invest for children's education. Investing money 'in trust for' children is another frequently used strategy with none of the conditions associated with RESPs.

Finally, RESPs represent another example of planning for the future. Parents and grandparents use these products in order to offset the financial burden of college or university for their beneficiaries. A little bit of money invested each month or year for a period of years is much easier to do, than to try and find large lump sums later when the money is needed, all of a sudden.

I've had many families tell me over the years that finding the money to finance college or university costs are next to impossible without some kind of disciplined investment program. RESPs are a convenient and simple means of setting aside money, on a lump sum or monthly basis, toward these expensive years for kids.

19

Why Are Adults So Concerned About Money and Financial Security?

Money is one of those topics in life that for some is the source of stress and for others indifference. Why is it that some people become highly frustrated with the notion of money and others couldn't care less about it?

There are many factors at play here beginning initially with the attitudes we inherited about money from our parents. For generations before us, concerns about financial security may be traced back to the Depression of the 1930s where bankruptcies were common and investment values plummeted. The goal of financial security evaporated for a whole generation of people for most of a decade and beyond.

Many grew up in families struggling to have enough to pay for basic necessities, leaving lasting insecure impressions on the mindset of the next generation. All facets of society were impacted by the Depression in some significant way. Raising the next generation with an awareness of the importance of spending and investing cautiously became a priority, after such a devastating period in history. The worries and associated stress lingers still in those that followed and is present in many of us living today.

Money is truly a necessary evil. We need it to live whether we like it or not. And while there is no direct connection between money and happiness, it is fair to say that one's level of comfort and quality of life is partially determined by one's income situation and net worth. Since most material possessions cost money, this is an inescapable reality.

For those with large amounts of money, either because of successful investing or wealthy parents, concerns about financial security may disappear. Others be come obsessed with money and financial security even though they may be wealthy in part, to avoid losing it, but also because they begin thinking of how to provide for the next generation.

If adults appear concerned about money and financial security, it is because they are concerned about having enough of it to maintain their quality of life and anticipated expenses in the future. They feel the burden and responsibilities of having to look after themselves and their loved ones not only in the moment, but well into the future, and this 'provider' mindset is one that lasts in most cases for a lifetime. After that, the burden transfers to the next generation and so this preoccupation with money and financial security continues.

If money was freely available and we could all be assured of a financially secure future, then our financial concerns would not exist. However in the real world, we need to earn a living, make money and provide a quality of life for our loved ones and ourselves. We buy food, clothes, homes, cars, kids go to university and the funding of a retirement capital pool seems a never-ending process. Using money and investments wisely is vital to feeling confident about your comfort and life options. Considering all of this, it is small wonder that adults often seem preoccupied with money, financial security and what it takes to build it. Few of us are ever taught how to invest money wisely. As in life itself, we learn a great deal through our mistakes; a learning process which continues throughout our lifetime.

20

What Does it Take to Build a Million Dollars?

The three main factors in addressing this question are: timeframe, amount of money and average rate of return.

If I'm 15 years old and want a million dollars when I'm 50, I would be able to achieve this with any of the following scenarios, assuming the following compounding growth rates of return could be achieved.

- Invest $1,375 per month (till age 50) averaging 3% per year

- Invest $750 per month (till age 50) averaging 6% per year
- Invest $375 per month (till age 50) averaging 9% per year

Or, invest a one-time upfront lump sum of $375,000 averaging 3% per year, or a one-time upfront lump sum of $49,000 averaging 9% per year.

As you can see, if the anticipated average rate of return is lower, the amount invested must be higher, to compensate for the lower return. Accordingly, if the anticipated average rate of return is higher, the amount you need to invest to reach your goal will be lower.

True, very few teenagers can afford to invest these amounts per month. Similarly, there aren't too many teens walking around with $49,000 or $375,000 to invest as a lump sum amount. The point here isn't whether you have a lot of money to invest, but to appreciate that by putting whatever you have to invest to work as early and productively as possible, you may look forward to building a substantial sum of money later in life.

Perhaps more realistic investment patterns for teens to consider would be as follows:

- Investing $50 per month averaging 6% per year gives me $179,813 when I'm 65 years old.
- Investing $100 per month averaging 6% per year gives me $359,625 when I'm 65 years old.

Remember that as we age and secure regular income from employment, our ability to invest larger amounts becomes more possible. The real lessons from this chapter are twofold:

- Invest as much as you can beginning as early as possible to maximize money (capital) growth.
- Invest as productively as possible keeping in mind the higher year-to-year volatility that goes with higher longterm average rates of return.

As mentioned earlier, the three magic ingredients for investing are time, amount of money and average rate of return. Ideally, with long-term capital building goals, we should try to make the most of all three of these powerful variables.

21

What I Wish I'd Known When I Was A Teenager

Permit me to share some of the thoughts that have occurred to me over the years as I reflect upon my youth.

- I wish I'd more frequently viewed my life as the gift that it is. If I had viewed my life as a sacred trust, my daily choices would have been more consistent with that gift, that trust.

- I knew even as a teen that money does not bring happiness, but I didn't appreciate that money, like water, food, like life itself, was a precious resource, not to be squandered.

- I wish I'd known that getting started early with investing, even small amounts every month, could result in a number of good things including; being able to pay for university, a car, a house, a wedding, travel or to lay a strong foundation for early retirement. Investing regularly in a disciplined manner, in good markets and bad, makes all the difference in the process of realizing your goals.

- I would have been further ahead if I'd worked with a financial planner or investment advisor in my teens and benefitted from their counsel from day one.

- Time well used is an incomparable ally, yet time wasted can derail the best of plans. This is as true with your school studies as it is with investing. Moments in a day are gifts – time is one of the greatest gifts of our lives (just ask anyone without much time left) and when opportunities pass to use time wisely, frustration builds. This applies to all things, not just investing. Spending time with loved ones, reading a good book, enjoying your hobbies and developing your passions are all about using this journey called life wisely.

• Resolve to challenge yourself mentally and physically every day and make time for play. Your life is primarily about learning about yourself and the world around you. Doing things the easy way is never as satisfying as challenging yourself. We tend to learn more from things we try and fail at, as opposed to doing only those things that come easily. You will become better in all you think, say and do by continually seeking self-improvement.

• Set goals for yourself in all areas of life that are important to you. If you want to make sure you spend quality time with family, friends, faith, keeping fit, ongoing learning, investing and other pursuits, establish realistic timeframes and make the goals measurable. If you want to spend time with family, identify an outing of some kind every week that would count as quality time together. If you have a religious affiliation, set aside time each week for that purpose. If staying fit is important to you, block off parts of each week for keeping in shape. If you have an amount of money you want to acquire by a certain age, then commit to a disciplined investment program with the help of a professional. In short, work the things important to you into your daily/weekly agenda. Your life will be far more rewarding if you do.

• Write down your goals and objectives and look daily/weekly at this list. If you write your goals down on paper and review them regularly, you will be far more likely to accomplish them. When you do this, you are commanding your mind that these things are important and then your brain goes to work finding ways to achieve them. If there are facts of life, this is surely one of them and it is very powerful.

• Be the best you can be in every situation all of the time. When you think about it, what's the point in coasting through life in half measures? In giving it your all, you'll never wonder about what might have been, had you realized your potential. Your life is not a dress rehearsal. It is what it really is every moment of every day and those limited moments and days are all you have. Make the most of them. Realize your potential and fulfill your dreams in all you say and do.

- Worrying rarely accomplishes anything. Act with your best intent and let things fall where they may. Remind yourself every day of the good things in your life and appreciate your blessings. A grateful, positive attitude will make all the difference.

About The Author

Murdoch Matheson is a certified financial planner with one of Canada's largest independent advisory and wealth management firms. He lives with his wife Mary Jane and their two sons, Brock and Ian near Gananoque, Ontario. His first book, '*Make Money, Not Mistakes – 30 Winning Ways to Secure Your Financial Future*' addressed important client questions on building financial security. Murdoch was motivated to write this book for young people, addressing questions offered by teens, hoping that with a measure of financial security and comfort, they would be able to focus on their passions and realize their potential.

'Book Ideas' Worksheet

_____

1) Idea: _____

Action Items:

_____

_____

_____

Follow-Up Date: _____

2) Idea: _____

Action Items:

_____

_____

_____

Follow-Up Date: _____

3) Idea: _____

Action Items:

_____

_____

_____

Follow-Up Date: _____

4) Idea: _____

Action Items:

_____

_____

_____

Follow-Up Date: _____

'Capacity to Invest' Worksheet

Monthly Income Sources:

_____ $ _____
_____ $ _____
_____ $ _____

A Total _____

Monthly Expenses:

_____ $ _____
_____ $ _____
_____ $ _____

B Total _____

A – B = Monthly 'Capacity to Invest' _____

Savings/Investments:

_____ $ _____
_____ $ _____
_____ $ _____

Lump Sum 'Capacity to Invest' Total: _____

'Financial/Investment Goals' Worksheet

Short-Term (under one year) Goal Examples:

Funding a bicycle, computer, gift, vacation...

Medium-Term (under three years) Goal Examples:

Saving for college/university, an extended trip, a vehicle...

Long-Term (three years or longer) Goal Examples:

Saving/Investing for future wedding costs, your first home, your retirement, a specific dollar amount by a certain date...

Action Step Examples:

- Invest $X dollars per week from my part-time job
- Invest 50% of my weekly allowance

- Make/Invest $X dollars per week doing odd jobs
- Invest annual gift money of $X dollars

1) Goal: _____

Timeframe: _____

Action Steps:

_____

_____

_____

2) Goal: _____

Timeframe: _____

Action Steps:

_____

_____

_____

3) Goal: _____

Timeframe: _____

Action Steps:

_____

_____

_____

4) Goal: _____

Timeframe: _____

Action Steps:

_____

_____

_____

5) Goal: _____

Timeframe: _____

Action Steps:

_____

_____

_____

6) Goal: _____

Timeframe: _____

Action Steps:

_____

_____

_____

Q&A Worksheet

What is important to you about 'building financial security'?

_____

_____

_____

What role do money and investments play in your life plans?

_____

_____

_____

What does 'building wealth' mean to you?

_____

_____

What connection exists between money, investments and your other life goals?

_____

_____

_____

Worksheet

Worksheet

Worksheet

Building Wealth For Teens, Answers To Questions
Teens Care About

Book Outline:
A brief outline of the book may be seen at
www.trafford.com/05-3051

Book Mission:
My primary goal in writing this book is to improve financial and investment literacy among teens.

Book Promotion:
I am exploring opportunities to promote awareness of the book through the education system, the media and other organizations. I am interested in suggestions regarding charitable fundraising initiatives and book promotion/marketing.

Book Feedback:
Feedback about this book would be most appreciated along with suggestions for new book ideas.

Author Contact Information:
I may be reached by using the following coordinates:

Murdoch Matheson

218 Island View Drive   Phone: 613.382.6748

Gananoque, On., K7G 2V5   Email: mnm2@cogeco.ca

Book Ordering:

- Individual books may be ordered online at www. trafford.com/05-3051 Volume discounts are available directly from the author.

- The book may be purchased for $15.50 exclusive of GST and shipping (volume discounts are available).

- Approximately two week delivery is required for orders under 30 copies, between three and four weeks for orders over 30 copies.

ISBN 1412080053-3

Made in the USA
Lexington, KY
12 February 2017